PIANO · VOCAL · GUITAR

BEST OF The Avett Brothers

Photo courtesy of the Avett Brothers

ISBN 978-1-4803-6070-9

7777 W. BLUEMOUND RD. P.O. BOX 13819 MILWAUKEE, WI 53213

In Australia Contact:
Hal Leonard Australia Pty. Ltd.
4 Lentara Court
Cheltenham, Victoria, 3192 Australia
Email: ausadmin@halleonard.com.au

Visit Hal Leonard Online at
www.halleonard.com

ANOTHER IS WAITING

Words and Music by SCOTT AVETT,
TIMOTHY AVETT and ROBERT CRAWFORD

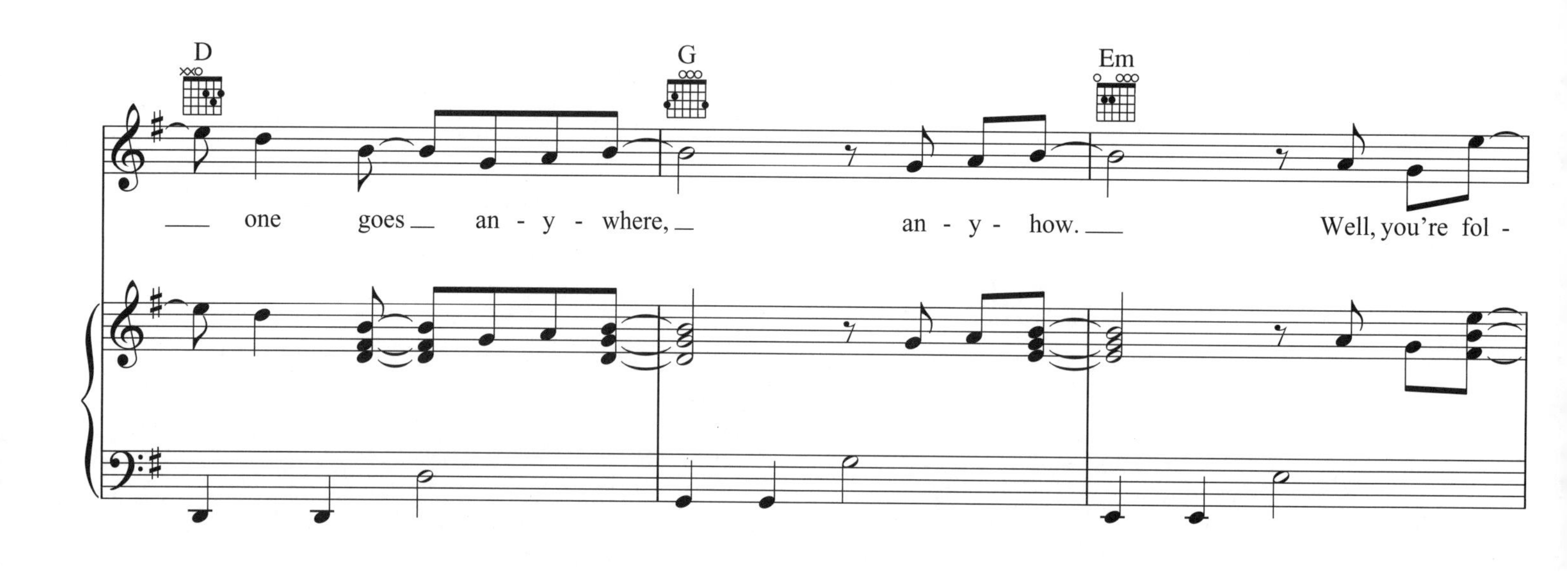

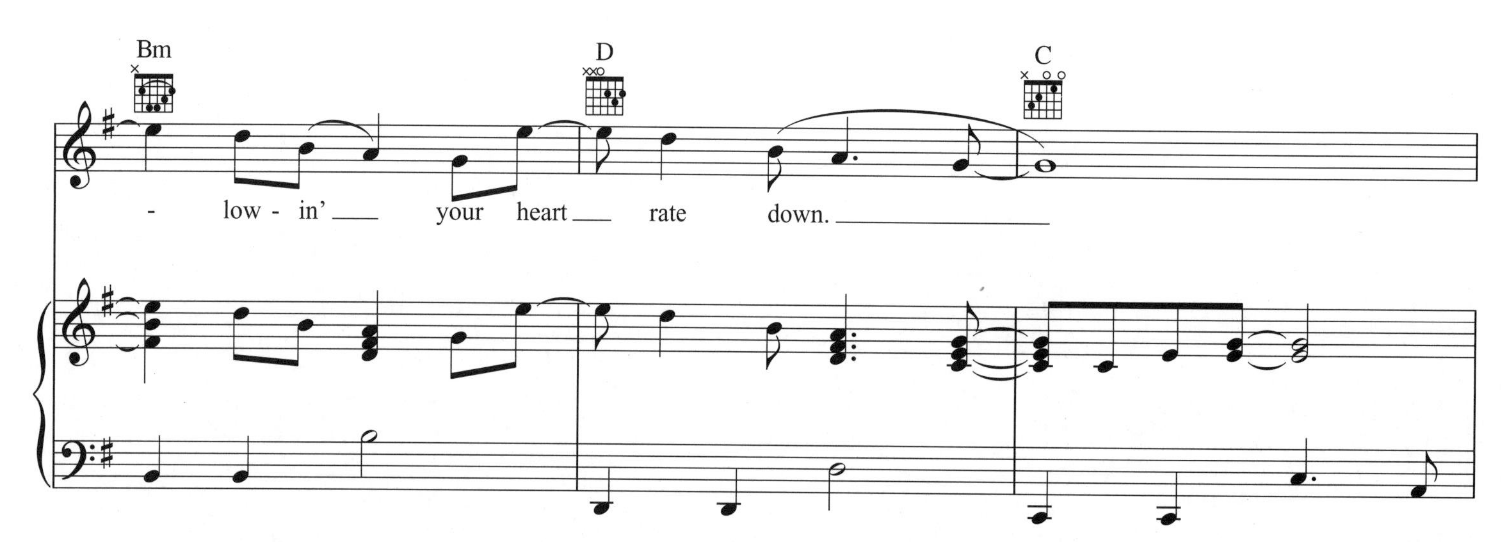

N.C.
She's a
G
Em
Bm
rose, she's a queen, but she's star - in' at a mag -
care, if you like, well, I'm stand - in' in the lan -
D
G
Em
- a - zine in the dark, on that path where they doc -
- tern light with our weap - ons and our love. And I use
3
Bm
D
- tor ev - 'ry pho - to - graph.
'em both to cov - er up.

C
G
C
An - oth - er is wait - in'.
She is - n't say -
G
A
C
- in' any - y - thing.
1
2
If you
But I love you
Em
and I care,
Bm
C
so you've got to get off that con - vey - or belt.

Em
Bm
C
If I could, I would come right in and take
you off my - self.
D
G
Em
Bm
It's a fake, it's a con, the na - ture of the road
you're on. Let me see your skel - e - ton well be - fore your life

D
C
is done.
An - oth - er is wait -
G
C
G
A
C
- in'.
She is - n't say - in' an - y - thing.
1
2
D
G

THE BALLAD OF LOVE AND HATE

Words and Music by SCOTT AVETT,
SETH AVETT and ROBERT CRAWFORD

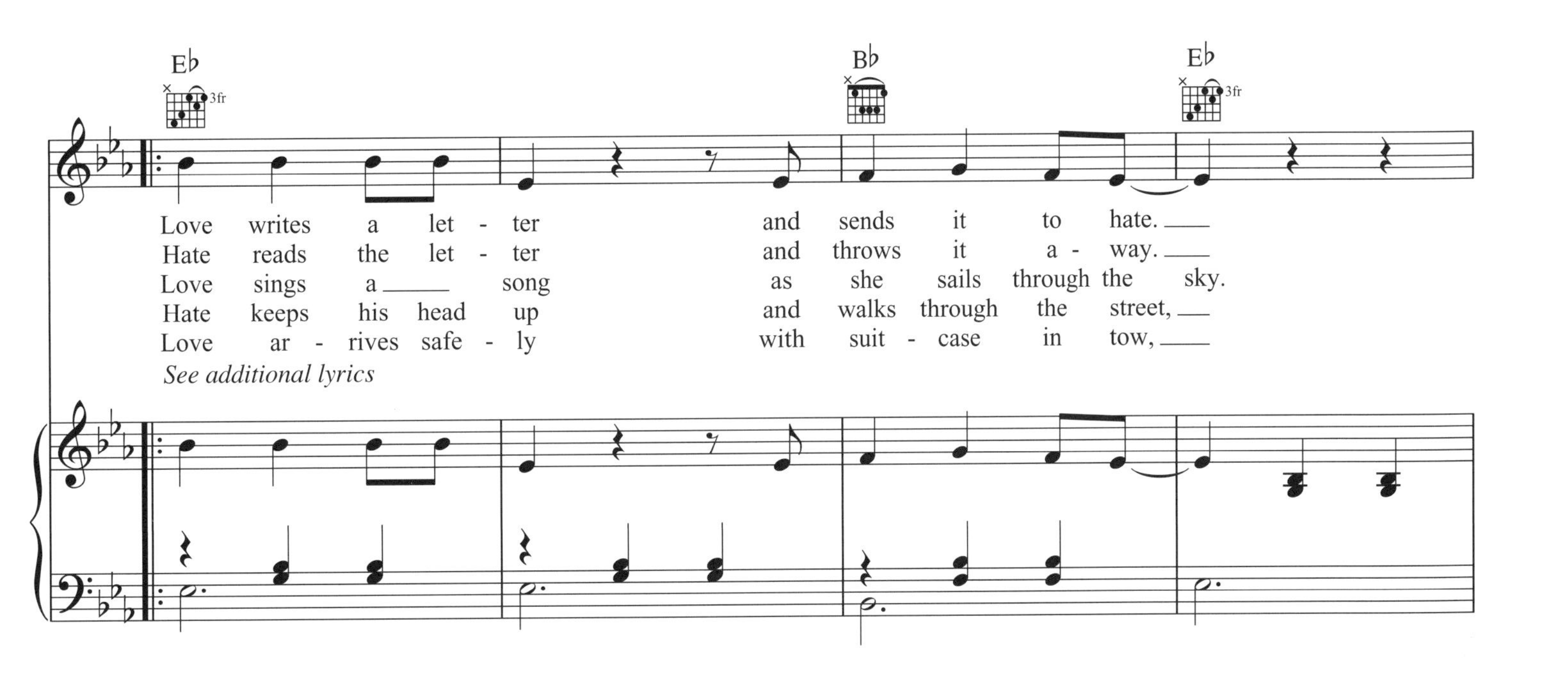

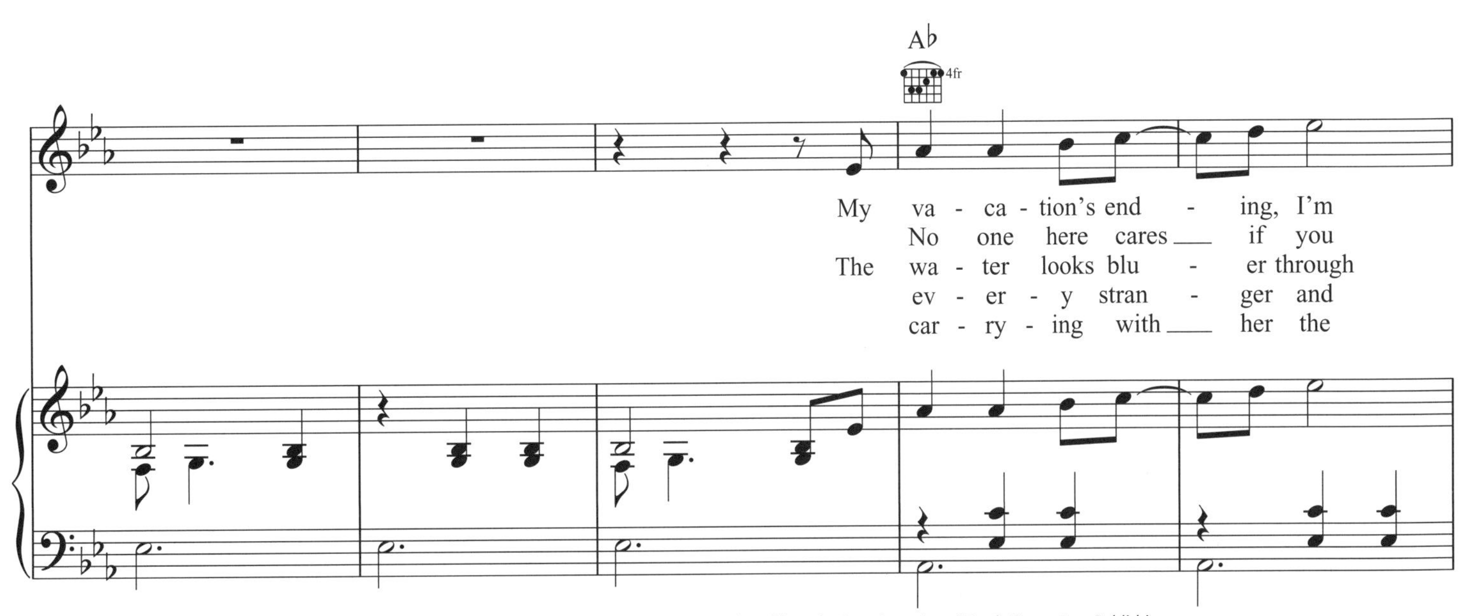

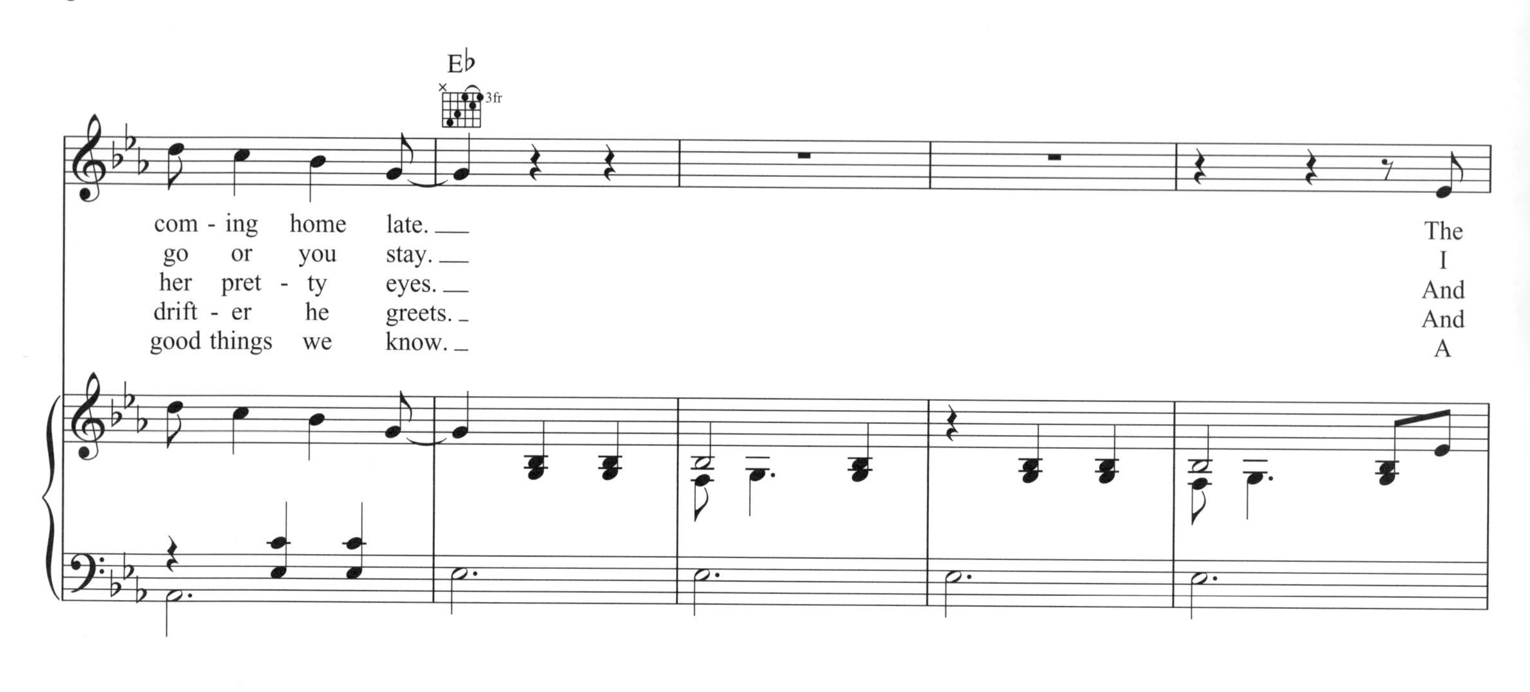
E♭
3fr
com - ing home late. The
go or you stay. I
her pret - ty eyes. And
drift - er he greets. And
good things we know. A

A♭
4fr
B♭
E♭
3fr
Cm
3fr
weath - er was fine and the o - cean was great. And I
bare - ly e - ven no - ticed that you were a - way. I'll
ev - 'ry - one knows it when - ev - er she flies and
shakes hands with ev - 'ry lon - er he meets with a
rea - son to live and a rea - son to grow, to

E♭
3fr
B♭
A♭
4fr
can't wait to see you a - gain.
see you or I won't, what - ev - er.
also so when she comes down.
ser - i - ous look on his face.
trust to hope, to care.

Additional Lyrics

Hate sits alone on the hood of his car.
Without much regard to the moon or the stars.
Lazily killing the last of a jar
Of the strongest stuff you can drink.

Love takes a taxi, a young man drives.
As soon as he sees her, hope fills his eyes.
But tears follow after, at the end of the ride,
Cause he might never see her again.

Hate gets home lucky to still be alive.
He screams o'er the sidewalk and into the drive.
The clock in the kitchen says 2:55,
And the clock in the kitchen is slow.

Love has been waiting, patient and kind.
Just wanting a phone call or some kind of sign,
That the one that she cares for, who's out of his mind,
Will make it back safe to her arms.

Hate stumbles forward and leans in the door.
Weary head hung, eyes to the floor.
He says "Love, I'm sorry," and she says, "What for?
I'm yours and that's it, Whatever."

BELLA DONNA

Words and Music by SCOTT AVETT
and TIMOTHY AVETT

Moderately fast

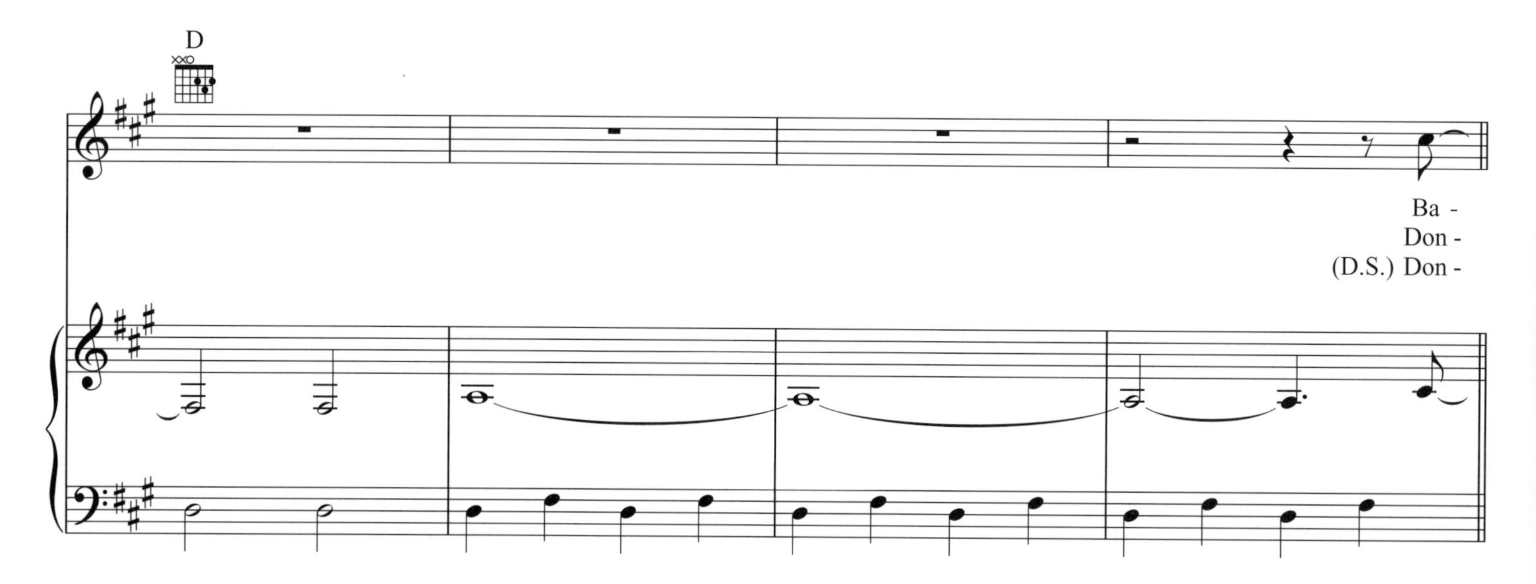

A
D
- by,
- na,
- na,
I asked you not to keep me wait - ing.
bel - la don - na, have you seen me?
bel - la don - na, are you lis - t'ning?
A
I told you not to keep me wait - ing.
Have you ev - er real - ly seen me
And were you ev - er real - ly lis - t'ning
To Coda
D
Now the af - ter - noon is fad - ing on.
like I want for you to see me now?
like I want for you to lis -
1
2
A
Lone - some, like you were

D
when you were six - teen,
when may - be e -
A
- ven I weren't lis - t'ning.
Did I help
D
when I was kiss - ing you?
D.S. al Coda
CODA
D
- ten now?

I AND LOVE AND YOU

Words and Music by SCOTT AVETT,
SETH AVETT and ROBERT CRAWFORD

G
D
G
One foot in and one foot back,
D
G
but it don't pay to live like
D
G
that. So I cut the ties and I jumped the tracks,
D
Bm
A
G
for nev - er to re - turn. Ah,

D
G
D
Brook - lyn, Brook - lyn, take me in.
Are
G
D
you a - ware the shape I'm in?
My
G
D
hands, they shake; my head, it spins.
Ah,
To Coda
G
D
Brook - lyn, Brook - lyn, take me in.

D
G
When at first I learned to
wom - an, she's got eyes that
D
G
speak, I used all my words to
shine like a pair of sto - len pol - ished
D
G
fight with him and her and you and me.
dimes. She asked to dance; I said it's fine.
1
D
Bm
A
Oh, but it's such a waste of time.

G
Bm
A
Yeah, it's such a waste of
time.
That
2
D
I'll
see you in the morn - ing time.
D.S. al Coda
Ah,
CODA
G
F♯m
Em

G
A
D
G
Three words that be - came hard to
D
Bm
A
say:
'I' and 'love' and
slower
G
D
G
'you.'
What you were then, I am to -
a tempo
D
Bm
A
day;
look at the things I

G
D
G
do.
Ah,
Brook - lyn, Brook - lyn, take me in.
D
G
Are you a - ware the shape I'm in?
D
G
My hands, they shake; my head, it spins.
D
G
Ah,
Brook - lyn, Brook - lyn, take me in.

1
2
D
Dumbed
G
D
down and numbed by time and age,
your
dreams to catch the world, the cage.
The
high - way sets the trav - 'ler's stage.
All

Bm
A
G
ex - its look the same.
Three
D
G
D
words that be - came hard to say:
Bm
A
G
'I' and 'love' and 'you;'
slower
a tempo
Bm
A
'I' and 'love' and
slower
G
'you;'
rit.
Bm
A
G
'I' and 'love' and 'you'.

FEBRUARY SEVEN

Words and Music by SCOTT AVETT,
SETH AVETT and ROBERT CRAWFORD

A
B
E
E/D♯
Soon - er than my fate
E/C♯
E/B
A
B
was wrote,
per - fect blade, it slit my throat and
E
E/D♯
E/C♯
E/B
A
beads of lust re - leased in - to the air.
B
A
B
When I a - woke, you were stand - in' there.

E E/D♯ E/C♯ E/B A B
E E/D♯ E/C♯ E/B A B
E E/D♯ E/C♯ E/B A
I was on the mend when I fell through.
B E E/D♯ E/C♯ E/B
The sky a - round was an - y - thing but blue.

A
B
E
E/D♯
I found as I re - gained
E/C♯
E/B
A
B
my feet, a wound a - cross my mem - o - ry that
E
E/D♯
E/C♯
E/B
A
no a - mount of stitch - es would re - pair.
B
A
B
But I a - woke and you were stand - in'

E
G♯m
4fr
F♯m
B
there.
E
G♯m
4fr
F♯m
B
There's no for -
E
E/D♯
E/C♯
E/B
A
- tune at the end of the road that has no end.
B
E
E/D♯
E/C♯
E/B
There's no re - turn - ing to the spoils once you've

A
B
E
E/D♯
spoiled the thought of them. There's no fall - in' back a - sleep
E/C♯
E/B
A
B
once you've wak - ened from the dream. Now I'm rest
E
E/D♯
E/C♯
E/B
A
To Coda
ed and I'm read - y, I'm rest - ed and I'm read -
B
E
E/D♯
E/C♯
E/B
- y to be - gin.

A
B
E
E/D♯
I'm ready - y to be - gin.
E/C♯
E/B
A
B
E
E/D♯
E/C♯
E/B
A
I went on the search for some - thin' real.
B
E
E/D♯
E/C♯
E/B
I trad - ed what I know for what I feel.

A
B
E
E/D♯
But the ceil - ing and the walls
E/C♯
E/B
A
B
col - lapsed,
up - on the dark - ness I was trapped.
And
E
E/D♯
E/C♯
E/B
A
as the last of breath was drawn from me,
B
A
B
the light broke in and brought me to my feet.

E
E/D♯
E/C♯
E/B
A
B
D.S. al Coda
There's no for -
CODA
B
- y. Yeah, I'm rest -
E
E/D♯
E/C♯
E/B
A
- ed and I'm read - y,
I'm rest - ed and I'm read -
B
E
E/D♯
E/C♯
E/B
- y. Yeah, I'm rest - ed and I'm read - y
I'm

A
B
rest - ed and I'm read - y
to be - gin.
E
G♯m
4fr
F♯m
I'm
B
E
E/D♯
E/C♯
E/B
read - y to be - gin.
A
B
E
rit.

HEAD FULL OF DOUBT/ ROAD FULL OF PROMISE

Words and Music by SCOTT AVETT,
SETH AVETT and ROBERT CRAWFORD

Moderately

G D C Em G D C

mf

Em G D C

There's a dark-ness up-on ___ me that's flood-ed in

Em G D C

light. In the fine print they tell ___ me what's wrong and what's

Em G D C Em

right. And it comes ___ in black ___ and it comes ___ in white. And I'm

D
C
fright-ened by those who don't see it.
When
G
D
C
Em
noth-ing is owed, de - served or ex - pect - ed,
and your life
dark ness up-on you that's flood - ed in light.
In the
G
D
C
Em
does-n't change by the man that's e - lect - ed.
If you're
fine print they tell you what's wrong and what's right.
And it
G
D
C
Em
D
loved by some - one, you're nev - er re - ject - ed. De - cide what to be and go
flies by day and it flies by night and I'm fright - ened by those who don't

C
G
C
be it.
see it.
There was a dream and one day I could
G
C
G
D
C
D
see it.
Like a bird in a cage I broke in and de-mand - ed that some-bod - y
G
C
G
C
free it.
And there was a kid with a head full of doubt.
G
C
G
D
C
D
To Coda
So, I'll scream till I die and the last of those bad thoughts are fi - nal-ly

1
G
D
C
Em
out.
G
D
C
Em
There's a
2
G
out.
C
Em
D
Em

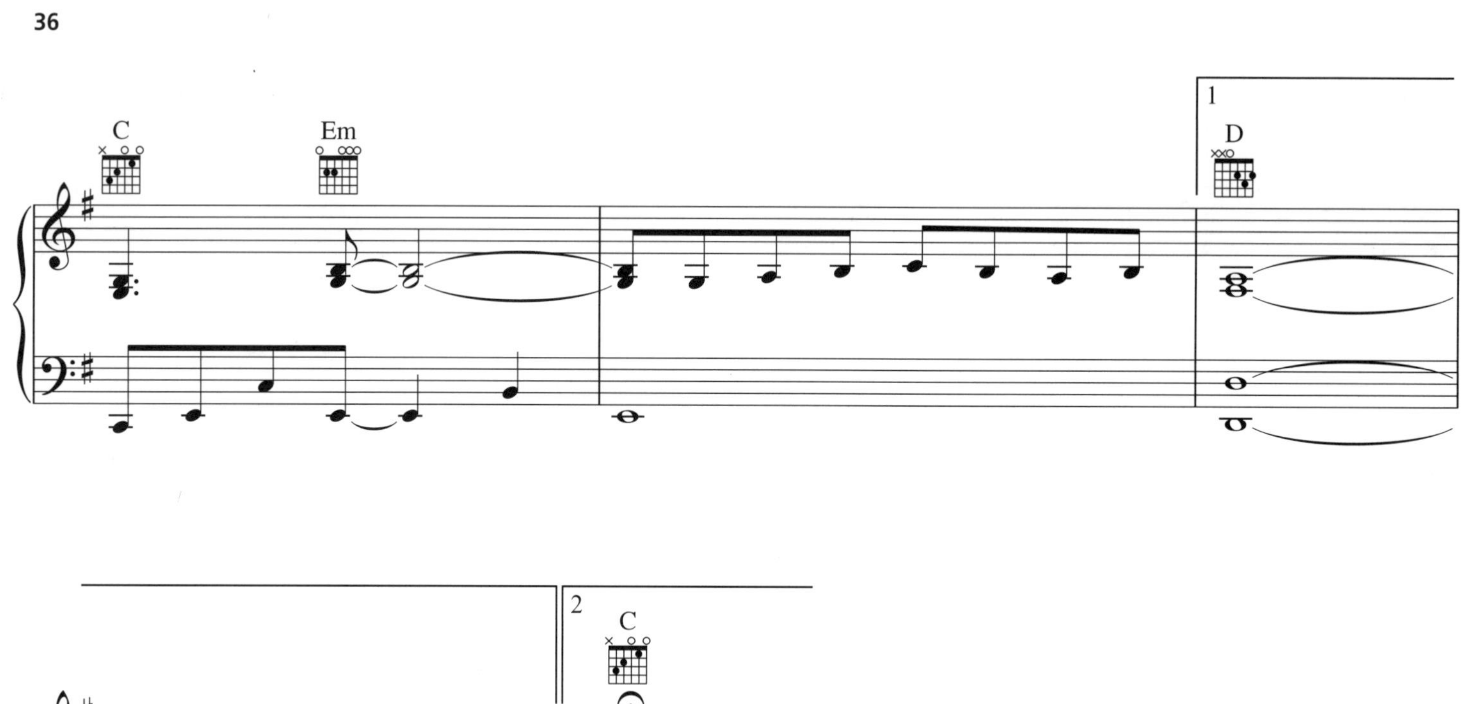
C
Em
1
D

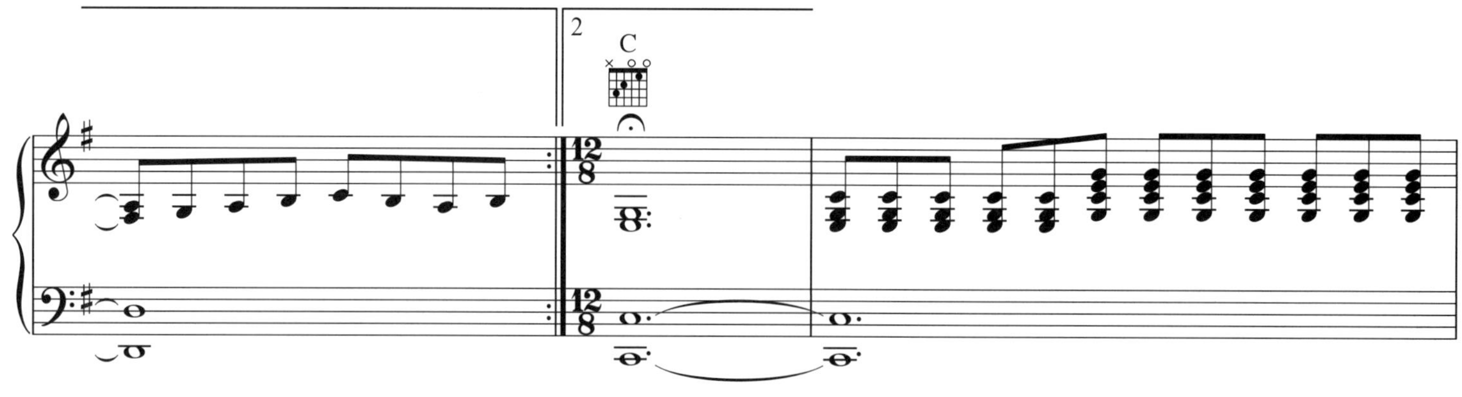
2
C

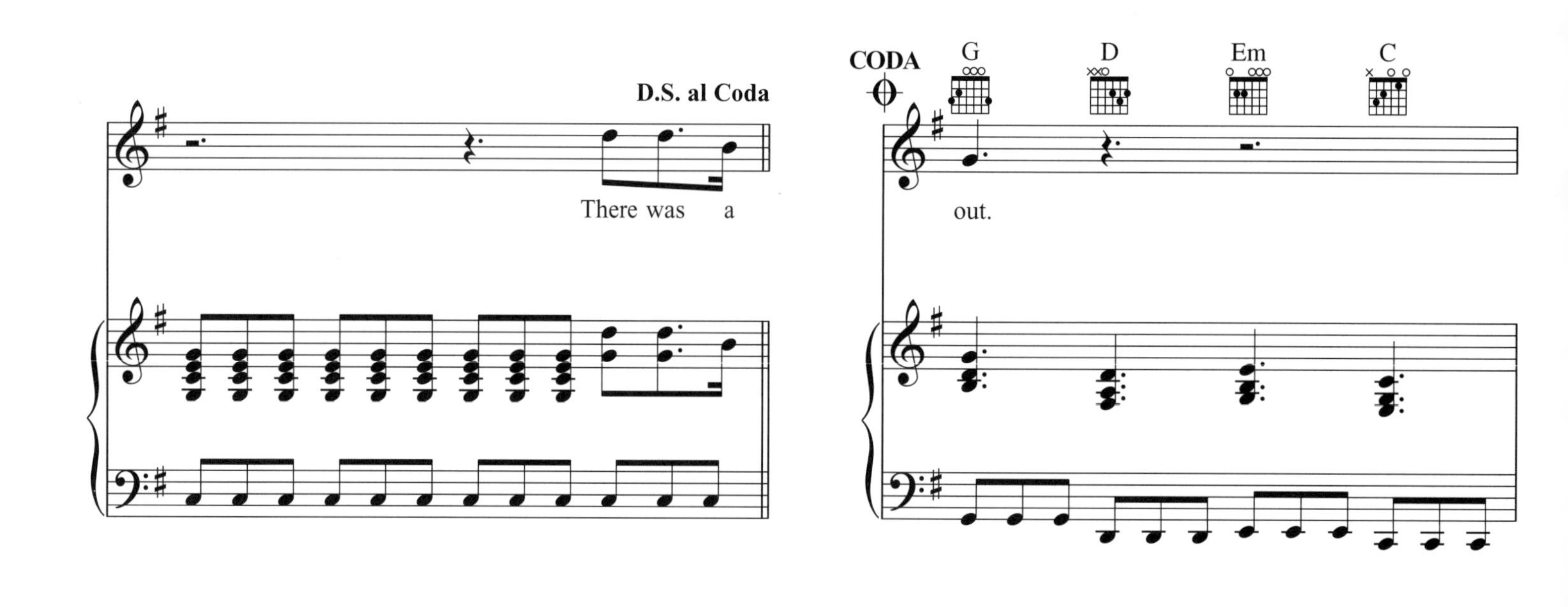
D.S. al Coda
There was a
CODA
G
D
Em
C
out.

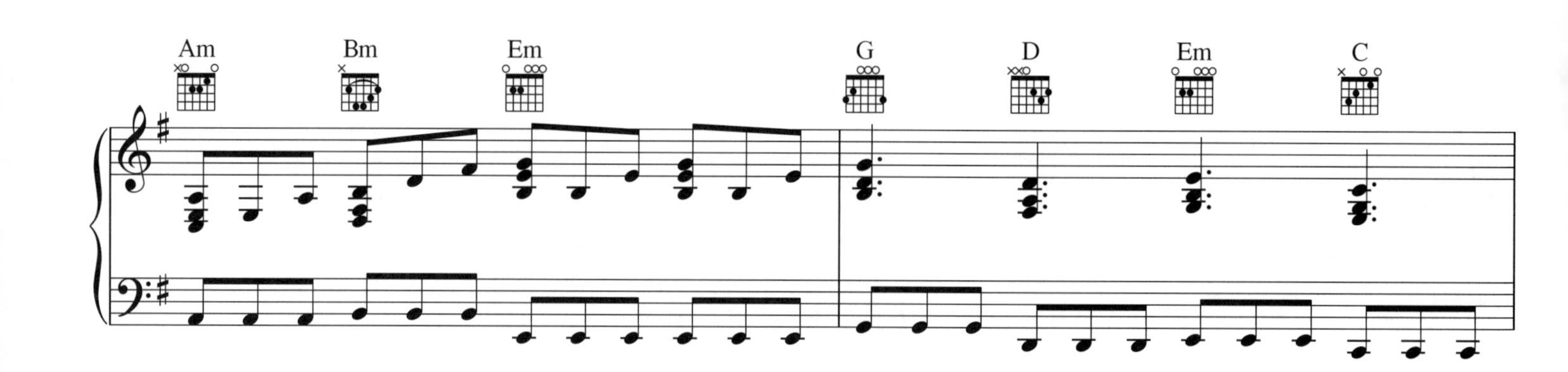
Am
Bm
Em
G
D
Em
C

Am
Bm
Em
G
D
C
There's a dark-ness up-on me that's flood-ed in
light.
In the fine print they tell me what's wrong and what's
right.
There's a dark-ness up-on me that's flood-ed with
light
and I'm fright-ened by those who don't see it.

I WOULD BE SAD

Words and Music by SCOTT AVETT,
SETH AVETT and ROBERT CRAWFORD

A♭
4fr
Fm
D♭
A♭
4fr
I would be sad be-cause the love I had be-fore.
Fm
I meant what I said when I said I would set-tle down
D♭
E♭
3fr
with you, al-though I know it's not some-thing that you were ask-ing me
A♭
4fr
Fm
to do. And I know we are young, but we won't al-ways be, so

D♭
E♭
3fr
mar - ry me. Let's not be that pre - dic - ta - ble young coup - le, chang - ing, mov -
A♭
4fr
Fm
ing on. But I can tell by watch - ing you that there's no chance of
D♭
E♭
3fr
push - ing through. The odds are so a - gainst us. You know most young love it
N.C.
Fm
D♭
ends like this. I would be sad be - cause you left me all a - lone.

A♭
4fr
Fm
D♭
Mm.
I would be sad be-cause the lies that you had told.
A♭
4fr
Fm
D♭
Mm.
I would be sad be-cause I got left by a
E♭
3fr
A♭
4fr
Fm
D♭
To Coda
girl that I a - dore. I would be sad for all the love I had be - fore.
A♭
4fr
I meant what I said when I said

Cm
3fr
D♭
I would re - ar - range my plans
E♭
3fr
A♭
4fr
and change for you.
Fm
You know me. I've al - ways been the kind with eas - y con -
D♭
- fi - dence. Con - fi - dent e - nough to hon - est - ly

E♭
3fr
A♭
4fr
be - lieve there's nothing out there stop - ping me, es -
Fm
pe - cial - ly not some - one who's not lov - ing me. Now
D♭
E♭
3fr
lis - ten here, I told you I could live on with - out lov -
D♭
- ing you. I was bluff - ing then, but it seems

E♭
3fr
A♭
4fr
that just might have been the truth. Well, my dad told me, "One
Fm
day, son, this girl will think of what she's done. And
D♭
E♭
3fr
hurt - ing you will be the first of man - y more re - grets
A♭
4fr
to come." And he said if she does - n't call, then

Fm
Db
it's her fault and it's her loss. I say it's not that sim -
Eb
- ple, see, but then a - gain it just may be.
N.C.
D.S. al Coda
I would be
CODA
Ab
I would be
Fm
Db
Ab
sad for all the love I had be - fore.

IF IT'S THE BEACHES

Words and Music by SCOTT AVETT
and TIMOTHY AVETT

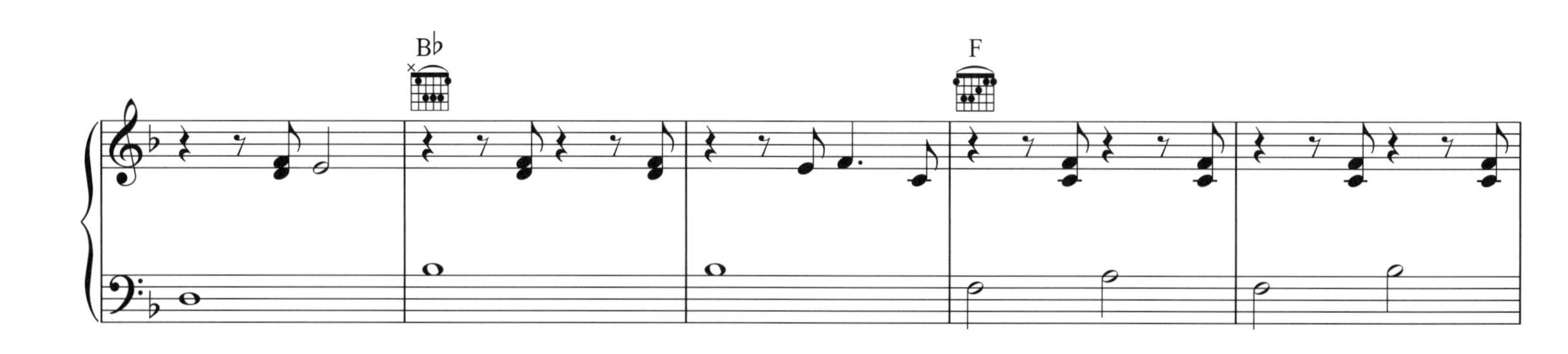

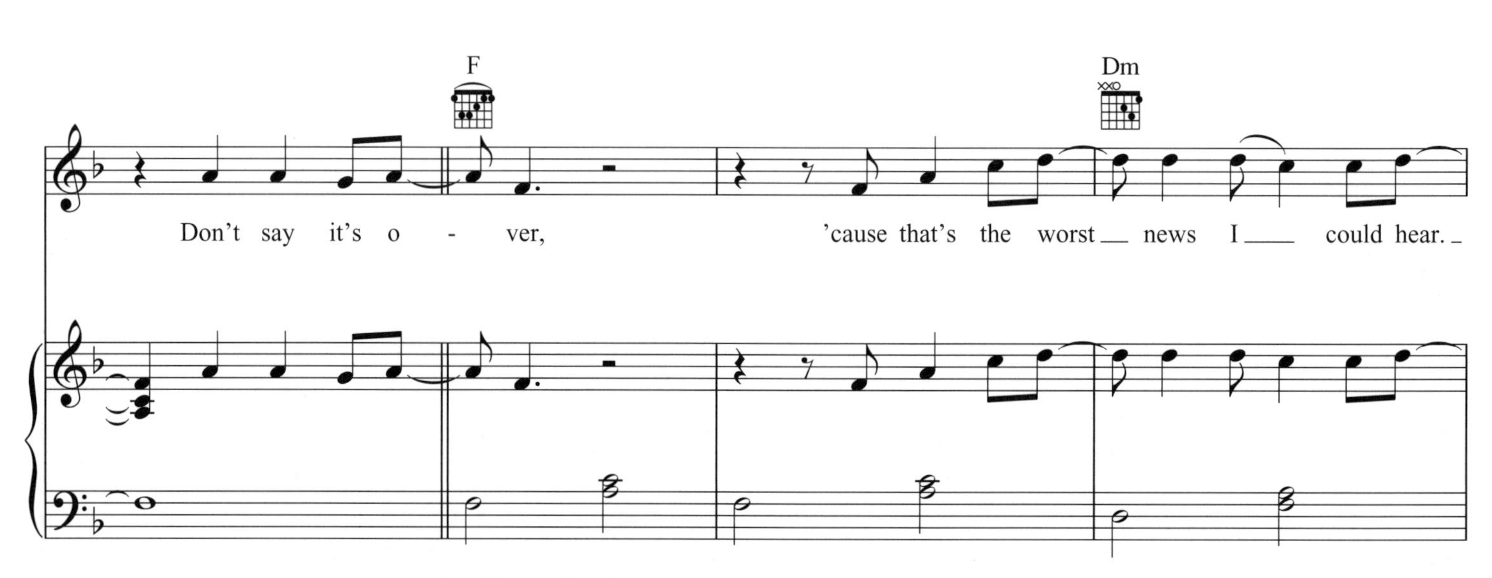

B♭
F
Dm
I swear that I will
do my best to be here just
the way you like it.
E - ven though it's hard to hide,
push my feel - ings all a - side,
I will re - ar - range my plans
and change for you.

Dm
B♭
F
If I could go
back, that's the first thing I would do. I swear that I
would do my best to fol - low through. Come up with

F
B♭
F
B♭
a mas - ter plan, a home-run hit, a win - ning stand, a guar-an - tee
F
B♭
F
B♭
and not a pro-mise that I'll nev - er let your love slip from my
F
Dm
C
hands.
B♭
B♭m

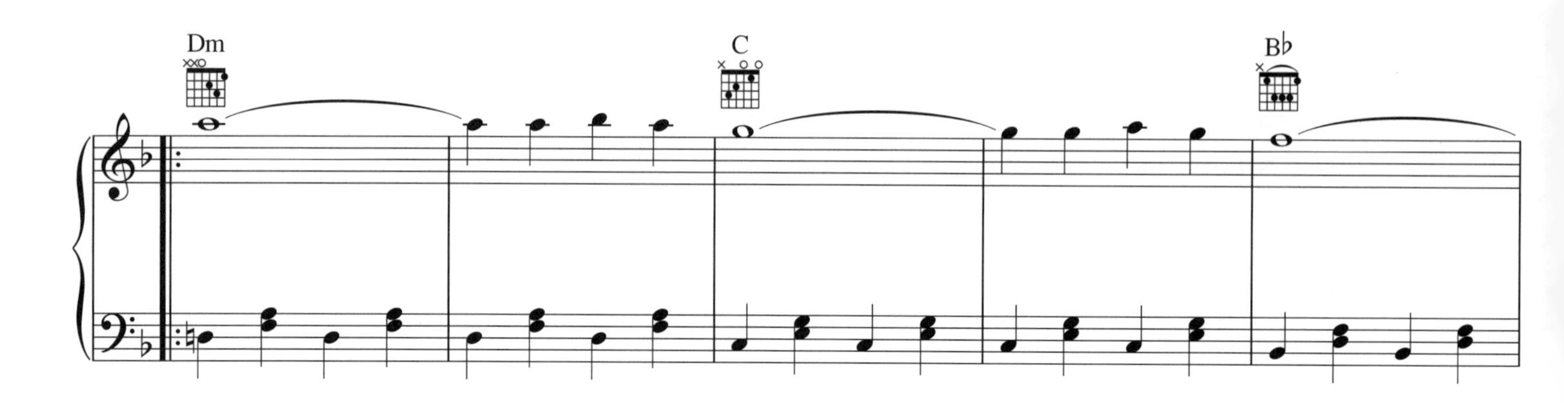
Dm
C
B♭

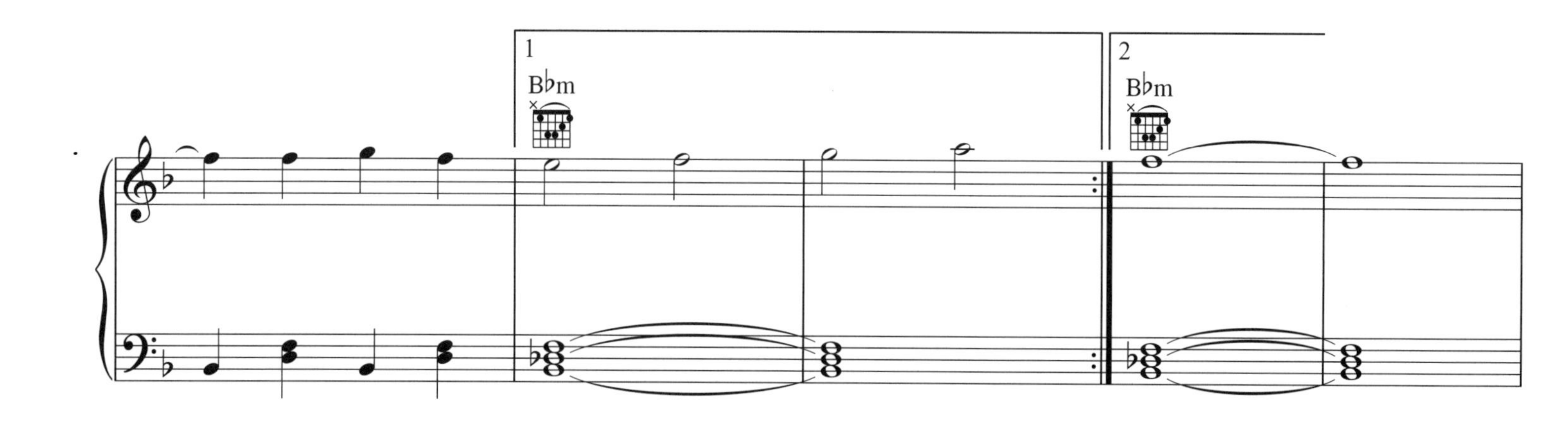
1
B♭m
2
B♭m

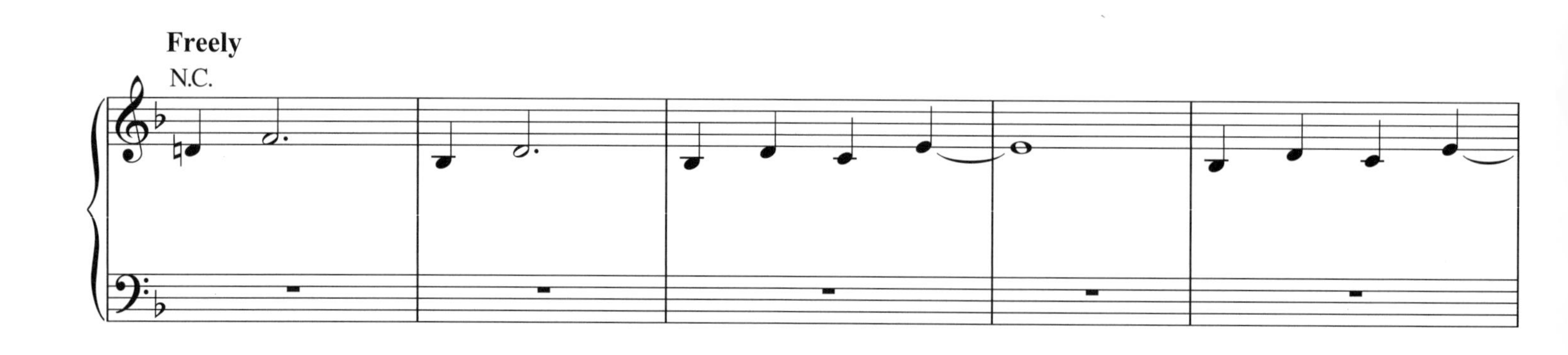
Freely
N.C.

To Coda
Tempo I
F

Dm
B♭
F
If it's the beach - es,
Dm
B♭
F
if it's the beach - es' sands you want, then you will have them.
Dm
B♭
F
If it's the moun - tains' bend - ing riv - ers, then you will have them.

Dm
B♭
F
If it's the wish to run a - way, then I will grant it.
Dm
B♭
F
Take what-ev - er you think of while I go gas up the truck.
B♭
F
B♭
F
Pack the old love let - ters up. We will read them when we for -
B♭
F
D.S. al Coda
(no repeats, take 2nd ending)
- get why we left here.
CODA
F

MURDER IN THE CITY

Words and Music by SCOTT AVETT
and TIMOTHY AVETT

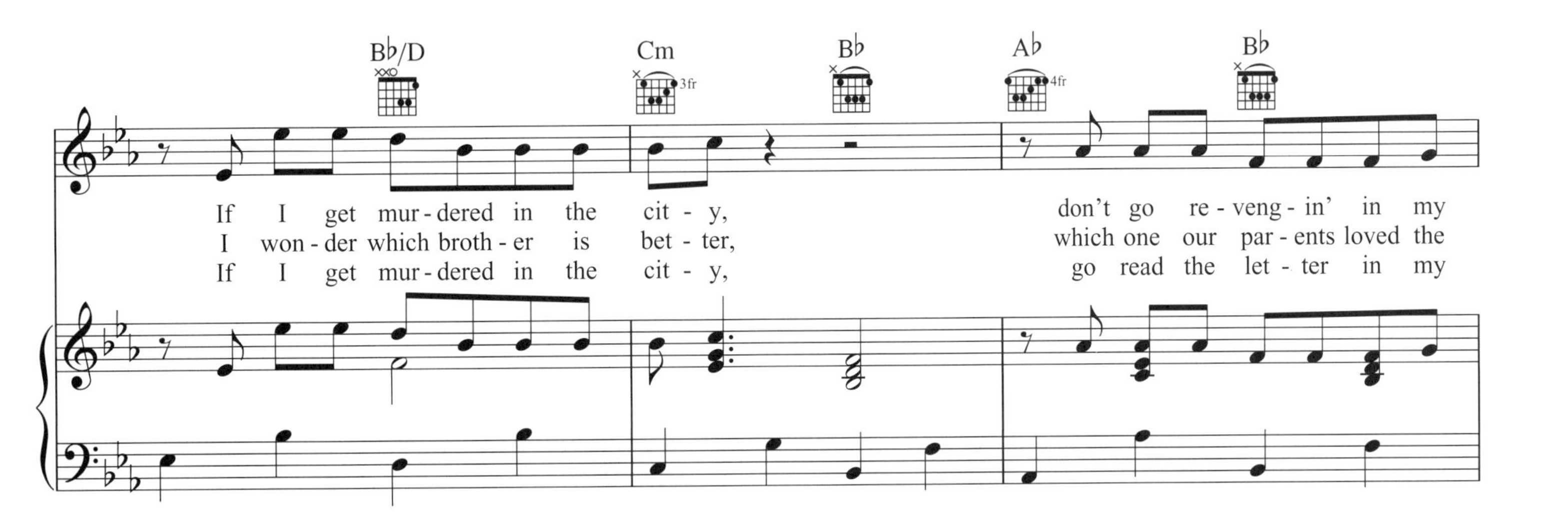

A♭ B♭ E♭ Cm B♭
4fr 3fr 3fr
no need to go get locked a - way.
They seemed to let the oth - er go.
But pay at - ten - tion to the list.
When I leave your arms,
A tear fell from my fa - ther's
Make sure my sis - ter knows I
E♭ Cm B♭ E♭
eyes.
loved her.
the things that I think of.
I won-dered what my dad would say.
Make sure my moth-er knows the same.
Cm B♭ 1 A♭ E♭ B♭
No need to get o - ver - a - larmed.
He said, "I love you and I'm
Al - ways re - mem - ber there was
I'm com - in' home.
2 A♭ E♭ B♭
proud of you both in so man - y dif - f'rent ways."

3
A♭
4fr
E♭
3fr
B♭
E♭
3fr
noth - ing worth shar - ing like the love that let us share our name.
Cm
3fr
B♭
A♭
4fr
E♭
3fr
B♭
Al - ways re - mem - ber there was noth - ing worth shar - ing like the love that let us share our name.
E♭
3fr

LIVE AND DIE

Words and Music by SCOTT AVETT,
SETH AVETT and ROBERT CRAWFORD

Easy Shuffle

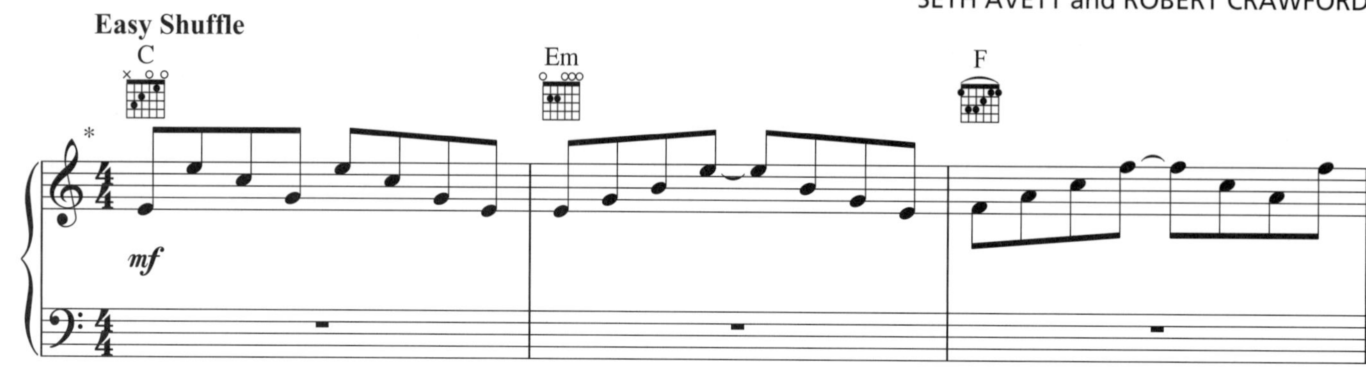

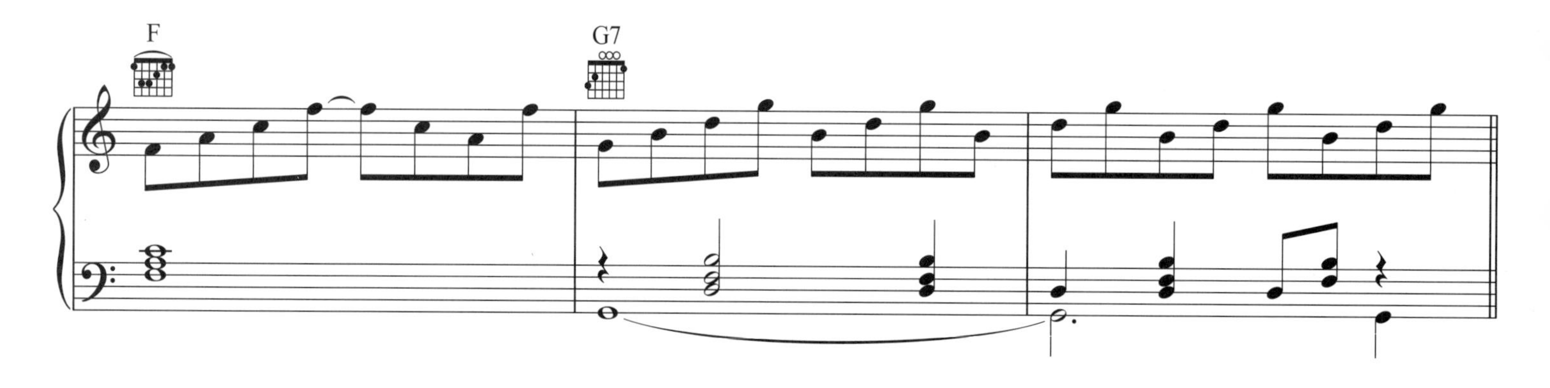

* *Recorded a half step lower.*

C
Am
you can say good - bye to how we
e - ven if there is no land or
F
G7
C
had it planned.
love in sight.
Fear like a hab - it,
We bloom like ros - es,
Em
F
C
run like a rab - bit out and a - way,
lead like Mo - ses out and a - way,
Am
F
through the screen door to the un - known.
through the bit - ter crowd to the day - light.
3

G7
Am
Solo ends
And I wan - na love you and more.
Dm
Omit second time
F
I wan - na find you and more.
Where do you re -
C
Em
F
side when you hide?
How can I find you?
'Cause
Am
Dm
I wan-na send you and more.
I wan-na tempt you and more.

F
C
Em
Can you tell that I am a - live?
Let me prove
Let me prove
Let me prove
F
C
Am
it.
it to ya.
it.
You and I, we're the same. Live and die,
Dm
G7
To Coda
1
C
Am
we're the same.
Hear my voice, know my name; you and I,
You re - joice,
You re - joice,
Dm
G7
we're the same.

2
C
Am
Dm
G7
I com - plain; but you and I, we're the same. You and I,
we're the same. Live and die, we're the same. Hear my voice,
know my name; you and I, we're the same.
D.S. al Coda
CODA
I com - plain; but you and I,

Dm
G7
C
Am
we're the same. You and I, we're the same. Live and die,
Dm
G7
C
Am
we're the same. Hear my voice, know my name; you and I,
Dm
G7
you and I.
C

LOVE LIKE THE MOVIES

Words and Music by SCOTT AVETT,
SETH AVETT and ROBERT CRAWFORD

Moderately fast

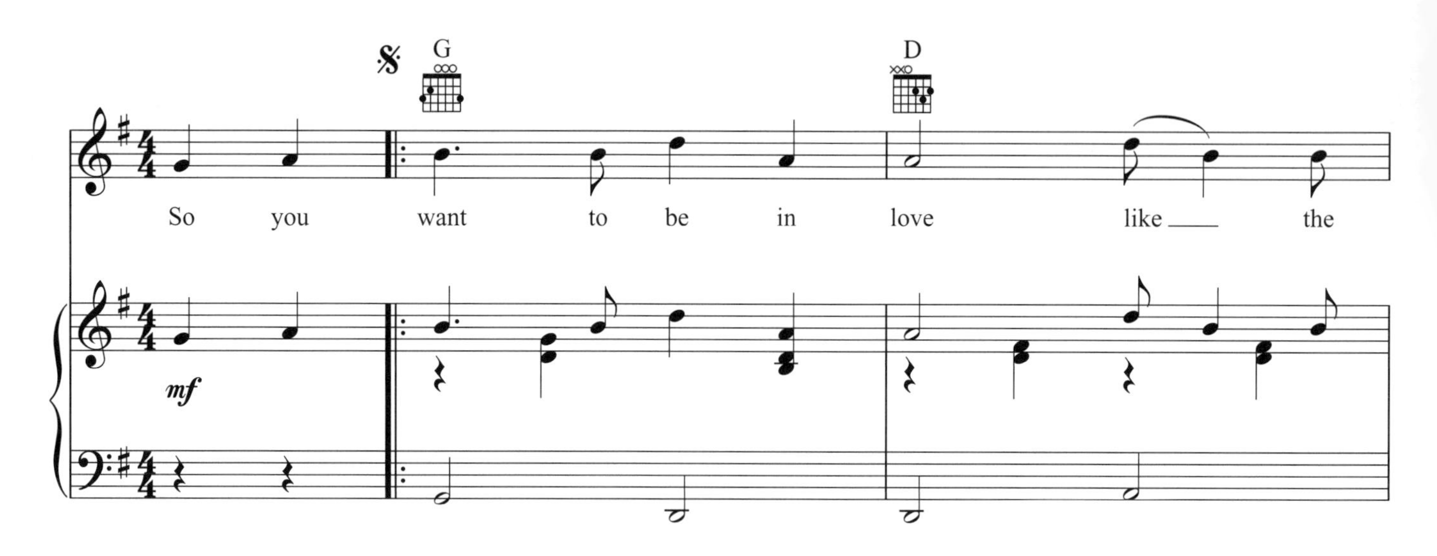

Em7
D
B7
twink - le in their eyes,
they're just say - in' their lines.
C
G
C
D
And so we can't be in love like the
G
To Coda
B7
mov - ies.
Now in the mov - ies they make
Well, you can freeze frame an - y
C
G
it look so per - fect.
mo - ment from a mov - ie
And in the
or run the

B7
C
G
back - ground they're al - ways play - in' the right song.
whole damn thing back-wards from reel to reel.
B7
C
And in the end - ing there's al - ways a res - o -
But I don't see one sin - gle sol - i - tar - y light tech -
G
B7
lu - tion. But real life is more
ni - cian or one sin - gle cam -
C
G
D
C
1
N.C.
than just two hours long. So you
'ra in this moon - lit field.

2
D.S. al Coda
N.C.
I don't
CODA
G
Em7
With a twink - le in their eyes,
D
B7
C
G
they're just say - in' their lines.
And so we can't be in
C
D
G
love like the mov - ies.
N.C.
G
N.C.
D
No, we can't be in
N.C.
C
N.C.
D
G
N.C.
D7
G
love like the mov - ies.

NOVEMBER BLUE

Words and Music by SCOTT AVETT,
SETH AVETT and ROBERT CRAWFORD

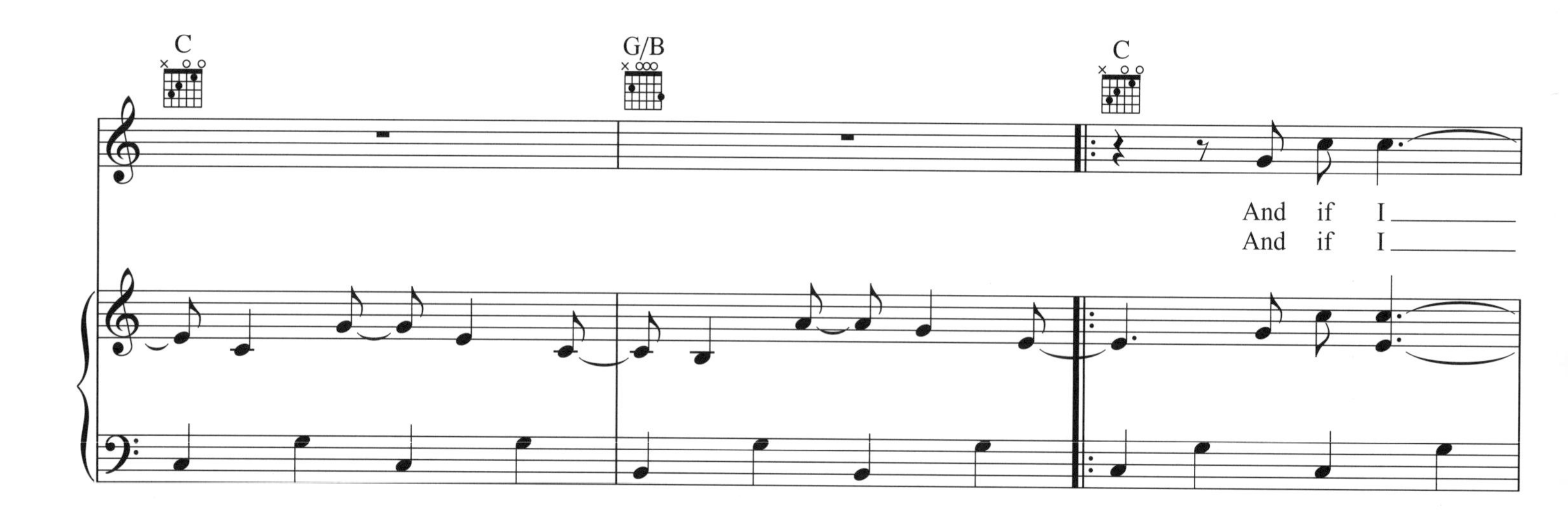

Am
G
F
G
C
would I catch you dream - in'?
would it all look good?
G/B
C
And if I were'nt gon - na be gone
And if I had a job
G
now,
now,
Am
G
could I
like a
F
G
C
take you home?
good man should?
G/B

C
G
And if I told you I loved you,
And if I came to you to - mor - row,
Am
G
F
G
would it change what you see?
and said let's run a - way,
C
G/B
C
And if I
Would you
G
was stay - in',
roll like the wind does?

Am
G
F
G
1
C
would you stay with me?
Ba - by, would you stay?
G/B
C
G/B
2
C
G/B
C
G/B
C
And my heart is danc -
And I don't know why I

G
Am
G
- in' to a No -
have to, but this man
F
G
C
G/B
vem - ber tune.
must move on.
C
G
And I hope that you hear it
I loved my time here.
Am
G
F
G
sing - in' songs a - bout you.
Did - n't know till I was gone.

C
G/B
C
I
No -
G
sing songs of sor - row,
vem - ber shad - ows
be -
Am
G
F
G
C
cause you're not a - round.
shade No - vem - ber change.
G/B
C
See, babe, I'm gone to - mor -
No - vem - ber spells sweet mem -

G
Am
G
- row.
Ba - by,
- o - ry.
A sea - son
F
G
C
G/B
fol - low me down.
blue re - mains.
1
C
G/B
2
C
No -
G
vem - ber spells sweet mem - o - ry.
A

Slower
Am G F G C
sea - son blue re - mains.
G
Your yel - low hair is like the sun - light, how
Am G F G C G7/B
ev - er sweet it shines.
C G
Bit by the cold of De - cem - ber,

Am
G
F
G
C
I'm warm be - side your smile.
Tempo I
G
Oh, la - dy, tell me I'm not leav - in'.
Am
G
F
G
And you're ev - 'ry - thing I dream.
C
G/B
C
I'm kill - in' my - self

G
Am
G
think - in'
I'm
fall - in'
F
G
C
G/B
like the
leaves.
C
G
I'm
kill - in' my - self
think - in'
Am
G
F
G
C
I'm
fall - in'
like the
leaves.
rit.

THE ONCE AND FUTURE CARPENTER

Words and Music by SCOTT AVETT,
SETH AVETT and ROBERT CRAWFORD

A
I ain't a gam - bler, but I can
F♯m
A
F♯m
re - cog - nize a hand and when to hold, when queens are
B
E
star - in' back at me.
C♯m
4fr
G♯m
4fr
C♯m
4fr
G♯m
4fr

C♯m G♯m E A B
E A F♯m
Once I was a car - pen - ter, and man, my hands were cal -
I don't come from De - troit, but her die - sel mo - tors pulled
A F♯m B
- loused. I could swing a met - al mal - let sure and straight.
me. And I fol - lowed till I fi - n'ly lost my way.
E
But I took to the high -
And now I spend my days

A
F♯m
A
- way, a po - et young and hun - gry and I left
in search of a wom - an we call pur - pose and if I ev -
F♯m
B
E
the tim - bers rot - ting where they lay.
- er pass back through her town, I'll stay.
A
For - ev - er I will move like the world
Am
E
that turns be - neath me. And when I lose my di - rec -

C♯m
4fr
B
-tion, I'll look up to the sky.
And when the black
A
cloak
dress
cloak
drags up-on the ground,
Am
I'll be read-y to sur-ren-
E
C♯m
4fr
-der and re-mem-ber we're all in this to-geth-er.
B
A
If I live the life I'm giv-

Am
To Coda
1
en,
I won't be scared _ to die.
E
2
won't be scared _ to die.
C#m
G#m
C#m
G#m
C#m
4fr
G#m
E
A
B

E
A
My life is but a coin pulled
F♯m
A
F♯m
from an emp - ty pock - et, dropped in - to a slot with dreams of
B
E
sev - ens close be - hind.

A
F♯m
Hope and fear go with it. And the moon and the sun go spin -
A
F♯m
B
- nin' like the num - bers and the fruits before our eyes.
E
F♯m
E/G♯
A
Some - times I hit, some - times
B
E
F♯m
E/G♯
it robs me blind.
Some - times I

A
B
E
hit, some - times ___ it robs ___ me blind. ___
D.S. al Coda
For -
CODA
won't be scared ___ to die. ___
E
N.C.
rit.
E

SWEPT AWAY

Words and Music by SCOTT AVETT,
SETH AVETT and ROBERT CRAWFORD

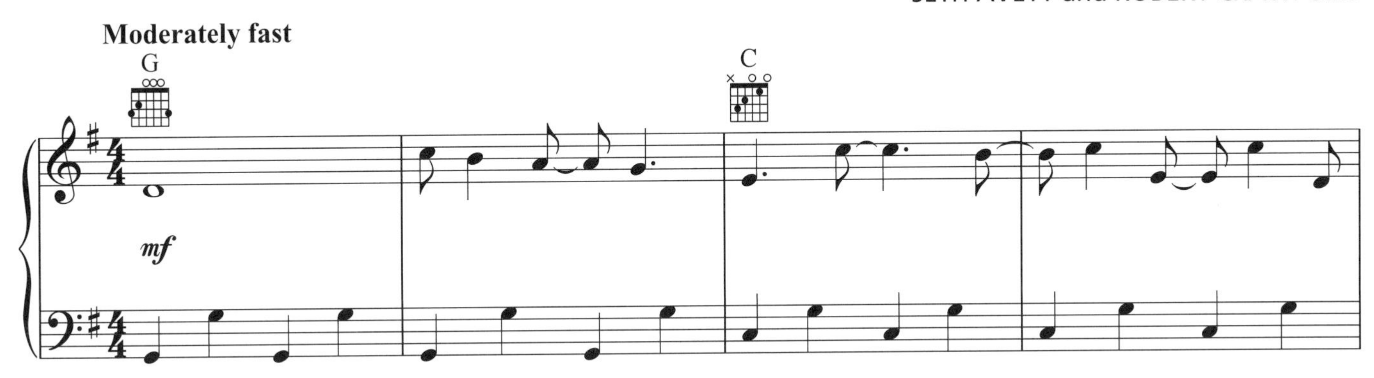

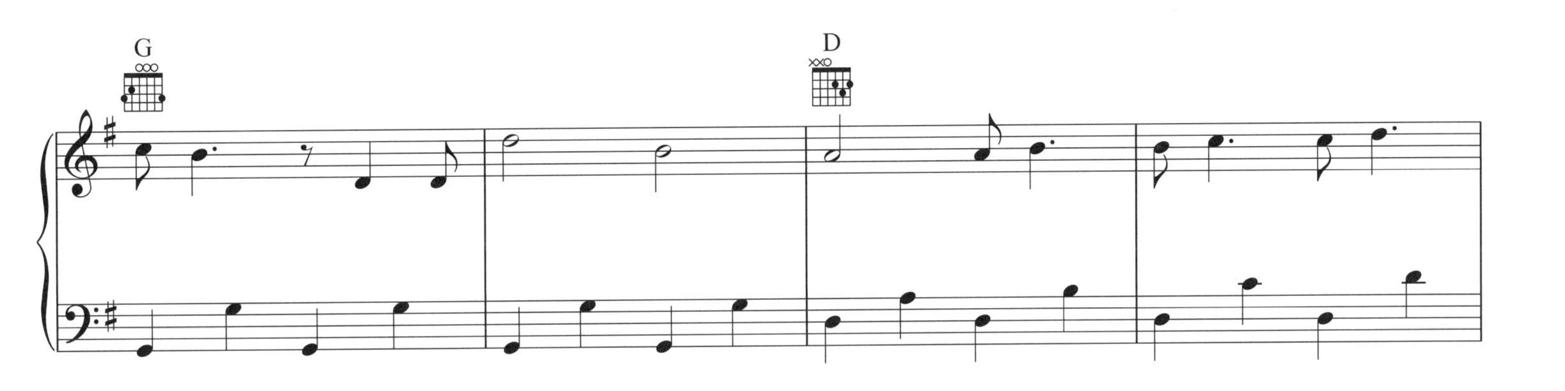

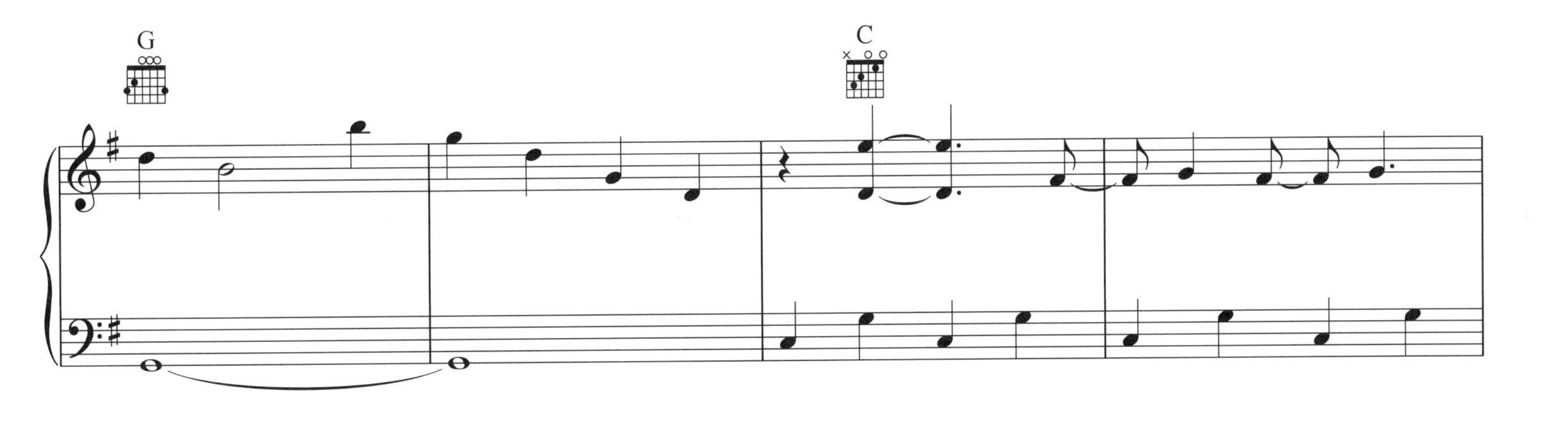

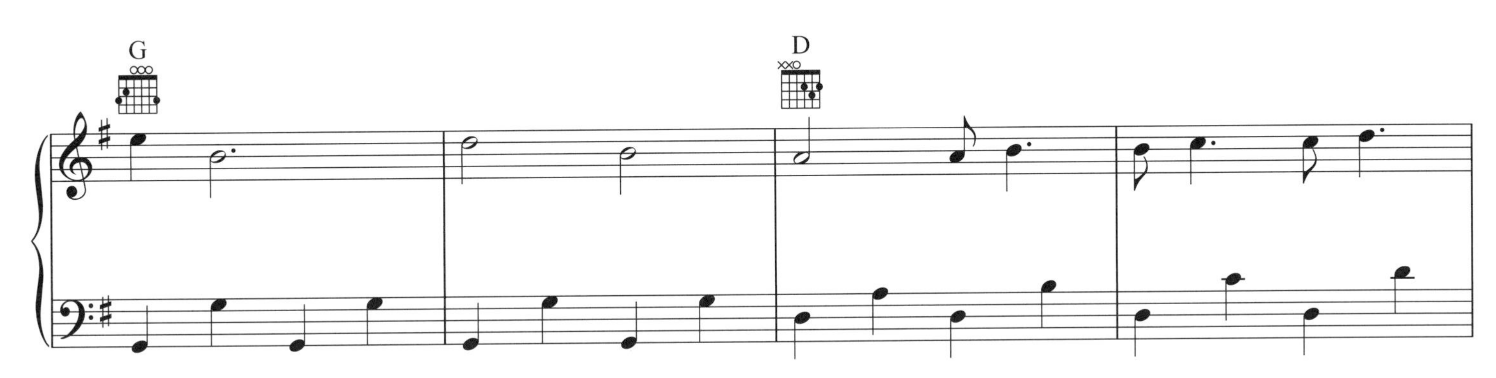

Em
C
G
Em
C
G
Well, you
C
send my life a whirl - in',
the end of the rain - bow. But
with such hon - est feel - ing, but
G
dar - lin', when you're twirl - in' on the floor.
what more is a rain - bow than col - ors out of reach?
what'd you real - ly mean when you said that I'm your man?

D
G
And who cares a - bout to - mor - row?
If you come down to my win - dow,
Well, how, my dar - lin', can it be
C
G
What more is to - mor - row than an - oth - er day
and I climb out my win - dow, then we'll get out of reach,
when you have nev - er seen me and you nev - er will a - gain
D
when you
then you
that you
Em
C
G
swept me a - way?
Yeah, you

Em
C
G
1
swept me a - way.
C
G
D
I see
2
3
You said
Life is ev - er chang - ing, but

C
G
I will al-ways find a con - stant and com-fort in your love.
D
G
With your heart my soul is bound.
C
G
And as we dance, I know that heav-en can be found.
D
G
Well, you send my life a whirl-

C
G
- in', dar - lin', darlin', when you're twirl - in' on the floor.
D
G
And who cares a - bout to - mor -
C
G
- row? What more is to - mor - row than an - oth - er day
D
Em
C
when you swept me a - way?

G
Em
C
Yeah, you
swept me a - way.
G
Em
C
Yeah, you
swept me a - way.
rit.
G
a tempo
N.C.
8va

TEAR DOWN THE HOUSE

Words and Music by SCOTT AVETT
and TIMOTHY AVETT

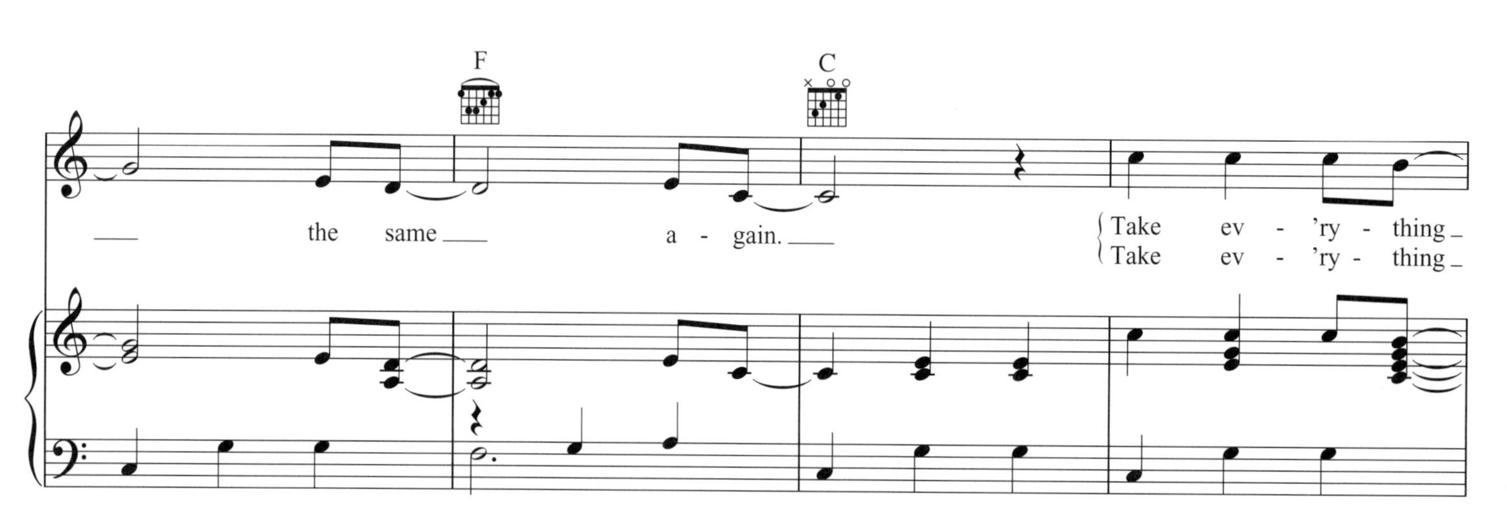

* Recorded a half step lower.

C/B
F
C
that I've collected, throw it in
that I used to own and burn it in
G
C
C
a pile.
a pile.
(D.S.) Bulldoze the woods
Park the old car
I remem-
C/B
F
C
that I ran through. Carry the pic-
that I love the best. Inspection's due
-ber cryin' over you. And I don't mean like a
F
C
-tures of me and you. I have no
and it won't pass the test. It's funny how
couple of tears and I'm blue. I'm talkin' 'bout col-

C/B
F
C
To Coda
1, 2
mem - o - ry of who I once was and I don't re - mem -
I have to put it to rest. and how one day
laps - in' and scream - in' at the moon. But
G
C
- ber your name.
I will join it.
3
F
C
I'm a bet - ter man for hav - in' gone through it. Yes,
G
C
I'm a bet - ter man for hav - in' gone through.

C/B
F
Ev - er since I learned how to curse,
C
F
I've been us - in' those sor - ry old words.
C
C/B
F/A
But I'm talk - in' to these chil - dren and I'm keep - in' it clean.

C
F
I don't need those words to say what I mean.
C
G
No, I don't need those words to say what I mean.
C
D.S. al Coda
CODA
G
C
I don't re - mem - ber your name.